CORN

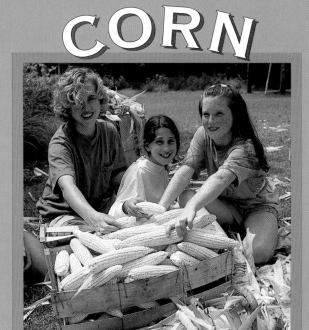

A TRUE BOOK

by

Elaine Landau

Children's Press®
A Division of Grolier Publishing
New York London Hong Kong Sydney
Danbury, Connecticut

Harvesting corn

Reading Consultant
Linda Cornwell
Coordinator of School Quality
and Professional
Improvement, Indiana State
Teachers Association

Author's Dedication
To Joshua Gramizo

Visit Children's Press® on the Internet at: http://publishing.grolier.com

Library of Congress Cataloging-in-Publication Data

Landau, Elaine.
   Corn / Elaine Landau.
      p.   cm. — (A true book)
   Includes bibliographical references and index.
   Summary: Examines the history, cultivation, and uses of corn.
   ISBN 0-516-21026-2 (lib.bdg)   0-516-26759-0 (pbk.)
   1. Corn—Juvenile literature. [1. Corn.] I. Title. II. Series.
SB191.M2L275   1999
633.1'5—dc21   98-47332
                                                                     CIP
                                                                     AC

GROLIER
PUBLISHING

Contents

Enjoying corn on the cob

Corn

Remember the last time you bit into a hot, buttery ear of corn? You might have been at the beach, a backyard barbecue, or sitting at the dinner table. You probably only thought about its delicious flavor. But there's actually a lot more to know about corn.

It might just be one of the most interesting vegetables you ever ate.

There are many ways to enjoy corn. It's often eaten on the cob or as loose kernels. But you may have eaten corn in other ways and not even known it. Corn is used in some syrups, cakes, breads, gravies, and pancakes. It is also an ingredient in many soups, mustards, chewing gums, jellies, jams, catsups,

Corn flakes are made from corn, of course, but bubble gum is also a corn product.

licorices, breakfast cereals, salad dressings, whiskeys, beers, chips, and puddings.

A hot dog with all the fixings may have a link to corn.

About 80 percent of the corn grown in the United States today—some 208 million tons— is used to feed farm animals, or livestock. Therefore, you may have indirectly eaten corn whenever you had a hamburger or hot dog.

But what may be most surprising is that corn is also used in many nonfood products. Corn has been an ingredient in fuel, soaps, straws, crayons, batteries, toothpaste, mouthwash, explosives, glue, yarn, medicine, paper, building and packing materials, paints, and other items. The food and

Corn is an ingredient in many soap and paint products.

nonfood products containing corn now number in the thousands. According to the National Corn Growers Association, corn can be found in just about every-thing from peanut butter to shoe polish.

Its many uses make corn an extremely valuable crop. It is the single most impor-tant crop grown in the United States. Nearly half the world's corn is produced

in the United States. However, corn is a major crop in other countries as well. It's grown on over 325 million acres (131.5 million hectares) of farmland around the globe. Large amounts of corn come from China, Brazil, Mexico, Argentina, France, South Africa, Romania, and India.

A family in rural China gathers corn.

Kinds of Corn

There are thousands of different types of corn. All are members of the grass family. Depending on its type, a cornstalk may reach a height of between 3 and 20 feet (1 and 6 meters).

That stalk will have a number of long, slim, wavy

To gather pollen, kernels inside the ear of corn produce a clump of corn silk at the top.

leaves. A corn plant also has other leaves called husks. The husks surround the actual ear of corn. They protect the rows of kernels on the cob.

The different varieties (types) of corn are grouped into the following major kinds:

Dent Corn—In these ears of corn a dent develops at the top of the fully grown kernels. Large quantities of dent corn are

Dent corn is tough and better suited to feeding farm animals.

grown in the United States. It is mostly used as livestock feed and for industrial purposes.

Flint Corn—Flint corn, also known as Indian corn, is colorful! Its smooth round kernels vary in color from off white to reddish brown. Flint corn is also hearty. It stands up well against insect pests. And it can survive in cooler climates than most types of corn. Flint corn is eaten by humans, although it is sometimes also fed to animals.

These colorful ears of corn are often used as decorations during the Thanksgiving season.

Flour Corn—Like flint corn, flour corn comes in different colors. Its kernels may be blue, white, or other colors. Even thousands of years ago, flour corn was extremely important to the Indians of Mexico and South America. Its soft kernels were easily ground into flour. And this flour was a major part of their diet.

Maize, or corn, was an important crop in ancient cultures.

Sweet Corn—This corn was named for its delicious taste. Sweet corn is picked from the stalk before the kernels have fully grown. At that point the

A field of sweet corn

corn is especially sweet. Sweet corn may be yellow or white in color.

Waxy Corn—Waxy corn's kernels have a waxlike look. This corn was first grown in China. It was brought to the United States in the early 1900s. Waxy corn is used in some puddings, sauces, and jellies, and to make glue for envelopes and boxes.

Pod Corn—Some scientists think pod corn may be the oldest form of corn. Unlike other

corns, each pod corn kernel is wrapped in its own husk. The entire ear of corn is enclosed in husks as well. Pod corn is no longer grown for either food or industrial use. However, scientists still study it in laboratories to learn more about corn.

Popcorn—Of the major types of corn, popcorn is the only one that pops. There are different kinds of popcorn. These range in color from off white or light gold to red, black, and many colors in between. Once popped, popcorn has two basic shapes. One

Popcorn can pop 3 feet high in the air.

is the snowflake, which pops into large cloudlike kernels. The other shape is the mushroom, which pops into a ball.

Americans eat 17.1 billion quarts of popcorn each year. That's about 64 quarts for every man, woman, and child in the United States. Surveys show that nearly 70 percent of all popcorn is eaten at home. The other 30 percent is enjoyed at movie theaters, sports stadiums, and at special events.

A Sweet Treat

Popcorn Balls

Roll up your sleeves, wash your hands, and try a new way to make an old favorite— popcorn balls!

You will need:
1 package of microwave popcorn
1/2 cup margarine
1 package of mini-marshmallows

Pop the popcorn, with an adult's supervision, in the microwave according to the package directions. In a separate bowl, melt the margarine and marshmallows together in the microwave. Combine this mixture with the popcorn, and form it into balls, using your hands. These are sticky, so cover each one in plastic wrap before giving out to your friends.

The History of Corn

Corn has a long history. Several seven-thousand-year-old corncob fossils have been found. And it's believed that Indians living in Mexico may have gathered and eaten wild corn over ten thousand years ago. These ears of corn were quite small.

An ancient mural showing a cornstalk (left) and stones for grinding corn (below)

They were probably only about 1 inch (2.54 centimeters) long.

When Christopher Columbus arrived in the Americas, he found cornfields planted by the Indians. No one in Europe had heard of corn yet. But corn had long been a valuable food source for the native people.

The English colonists were introduced to corn at the first Thanksgiving feast in Plymouth, Massachusetts. Quadequina,

The first Thanksgiving in 1621 brought Indians and pilgrims together.

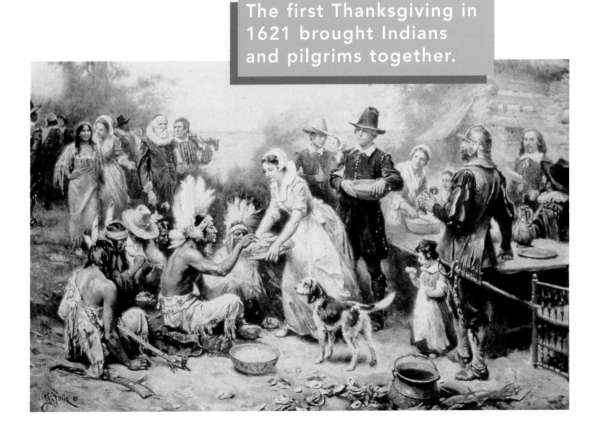

the brother of a Wampanoag Indian chief, brought a deerskin bag of popcorn to the feast as a gift.

With the Indians' help, the colonists learned to plant their own corn. This knowledge spread to other colonies along the eastern coast. Before long corn became an essential crop for these new Americans as well.

Sometimes the settlers used corn to pay their taxes or debts (money they owed). Often they

Early settlers ground corn using a plumping mill.

traded the corn they grew for other much needed household items. During difficult times, when there wasn't very much else to eat, corn helped keep them alive.

An A–maiz–ing Food

Corn was called "maize" by the Indians, and is still known by that name in most countries. Cornmeal was used by the early colonists to make a variety of breads, cakes, and fritters. Here's an easy recipe for you to make, with an adult's supervision, for your family.

Old Fashioned Cornbread

You will need:

1 cup of flour
1 teaspoon of salt
4 teaspoons of baking powder
2 tablespoons of sugar

1 cup of cornmeal
1 egg, beaten
1 cup of milk
1/4 cup melted shortening

Sift together the flour, salt, baking powder, and sugar. Mix these ingedients with the cornmeal. Combine the egg, milk, and shortening, and then add this to the mixed dry ingredients. Stir until moistened. Pour into a greased 9-inch square pan. Bake in the oven at 425° F about 25 minutes.

As large numbers of settlers headed west they planted corn there as well. By the 1800s corn had become a major United States crop. At that point harvesting the corn was much easier. That was largely due to the invention of mechanical corn pickers. These machines pick the ears of corn from the stalks, remove the husks, and deposit the corn into a truck or wagon. A machine called a

corn combine also does this, as well as shells and cleans the corn.

Today much of the corn grown in the United States comes from an area in the Midwest called the Corn Belt. The weather and soil conditions there are perfect for growing corn. The Corn Belt includes parts of Illinois, Indiana, Iowa, Michigan, Minnesota, Missouri, Nebraska, Wisconsin, Ohio, and South Dakota.

Women operating a combine harvester in the Corn Belt.

Better Than Ever

Through the years, researchers have tried to produce better corn. They've bred various types of corn to create new corns known as hybrids. The different hybrids were designed to grow more corn. Many are also better, and can withstand drought and insect pests. In some cases, the

As part of his research, this plant breeder (above) places a bag over the corn tassle. Grasshoppers (right) can do severe damage to corn plants.

results have been remarkable. Today's hybrid popcorn pops up nearly double the size of corn grown forty years ago.

Corn may have an even greater impact on the future. Some corn products are good for the environment. Cleaner burning fuel made from corn helps protect the air we breathe. That's because it releases less polluting fumes.

Thanks to corn, our cars run on fuel that is less harmful to the environment.

Corn products, such as lawn and leaf bags, disposable (throw away) forks and spoons, and golf tees can be completely recycled. These readily turn into soil-enriching compost.

However, this isn't the case with many of today's other plastic products.

In the future, corn may become an even more important food source as well. The world's population is expected to nearly double in the next thirty years. The development of special hybrid corns will allow farmers to greatly increase their crop production. This may prove extremely useful in feeding a growing world.

A hybrid corn field can be the beginning of a better world for millions of people.

Having lasted through the ages, corn has stood the test of time. And as its uses grow, it's likely to continue to do so.

To Find Out More

Here are some additional resources to help you learn more about corn:

Books

Bailey, Donna. **Farmers.** Steck-Vaughn, 1990.

Bial, Raymond. **Corn Belt Harvest.** Houghton Mifflin, 1991.

Fowler, Allan. **Corn—On and Off the Cob.** Children's Press, 1994.

George, Jean Craighead. **The First Thanksgiving.** Philomel Books, 1993.

Hunter, Sally M. **Four Seasons of Corn: A Winnebago Tradition.** Lerner Publications Co., 1997.

Llewellyn, Claire. **First Look at Growing Food.** Gareth Stevens Children's Books, 1991.

Peterson, Cris. **Harvest Year.** Boyds Mills Press, 1996.

Powell, Jillian. **Vegetables.** Raintree Steck-Vaughn, 1997.

Organizations and Online Sites

Green Giant Home Page
http://www.greengiant.com/

Learn about the history of canned niblets and cream style corn, play a vegetable scramble game, check out corn recipes, and visit the Commonly Asked Questions department.

Illinois Corn
http://www.ilcorn.org/

Introducing corn nonfood products such as Eco-Foam, the packing peanut made from corn, and Hydrosorb, the "Super Slurper," used in fuel filters, bandages, baby diapers, and ice packs. You can also consult the daily Corn Industry Update, and get information on corn growing in Illinois.

Kelloggs
http://www.Kelloggs.com/

The home page of the cornflake king features the Breakfast Edition of "The Cereal City Times," with links to Club K, the Trivial Trail, Smart Start, plus health news, and sports.

The Popcorn Board
401 N. Michigan Avenue
Chicago, IL 60611-4267
1-800-877-POPALOT
http://www.popcorn.org

This really fun site includes a Popcorn Calendar, showing how popcorn fits into every month of the year; the Encyclopedia Popcornica, telling you "everything you've always wanted to know about the history and science of popcorn, but were too busy eating to ask"; a Cornucopia of Ideas for Teachers, and lots more.

Important Words

cob the hard center portion of an ear of corn. The corn's kernels grow on the cob.

compost a mixture of decaying vegetable matter used as fertilizer

drought a long period of dry weather

essential necessary or highly important

fumes poisonous or bad-smelling smoke or vapor

husks the leaves covering a corncob

hybrid a type of corn created through careful breeding

impact to have an important effect on

ingredient something that is part of or goes into a mixture

nonfood something that cannot be eaten

pollute to make unclean or impure

Index

Meet the Author

Elaine Landau worked as a newspaper reporter, an editor, and a youth services librarian before becoming a full-time writer. She has written more than one hundred nonfiction books for young people, including True Books on dinosaurs, animals, countries, and food.

Ms. Landau, who has a bachelor's degree in English and journalism from New York University and a master's degree in library and information science from Pratt Institute, lives in Florida with her husband and son.